Praise for Marie Nazon

In *What a Woman Wants* Marie Nazon brings to life the voice of women around the world. As I read this compilation, it not only reminded me of those things that matter to me and what I want as a woman, but stirred my imagination into thinking outside of the box of what I think I want and give myself permission to want "more." These voices come together as an orchestral piece resounding with laughter, tears, screams, and the softness of women unheard, yet standing now resolutely in a crescendo, unabashed and pleading to be seen in her authentic Divine Feminine self. It serves to remind me that I am not alone, and I have much more in common with my sisters around the world than that which seemingly differentiates us from each other. Pick up this book now, read and listen, and dare to speak your truth!

—Rev Julie MacDonald,
author of *The Evolution of The Spirit of Mankind*

What a Woman Wants will move your heart, spirit, and mind. It will turn you on and up, only in the way that the Divine Feminine can. I feel privileged to know the magnificent Marie Nazon and to be a part of one of her circles. There are no limits to the wonders of what a woman can do and the depth of our highs, lows, strengths, and challenges. They are captured here beautifully, and each page will remind you of something in or for yourself -or- of a woman whose voice rings loud and clear in these words.

—Alicia Holmes,
Financial Educator/Investor – Founder of Journey to Wealth

What a Woman Wants...

A GATHERING OF AUTHENTIC WOMEN'S DESIRES:
PROFOUND, FUNNY, EROTIC, POWERFUL, SPIRITUAL,
PROVOCATIVE AND SOVEREIGN SISTERHOOD

MARIE C. NAZON, PhD

Foreword by ALisa Starkweather

Copyright © 2021 Marie C. Nazon. All rights reserved.

No part of this publication shall be reproduced, transmitted, or sold in whole or in part in any form without prior written consent of the Author, except as provided by the United States of America copyright law. Any unauthorized usage of the text without express written permission of the publisher is a violation of the author's copyright and is illegal and punishable by law. All trademarks and registered trademarks appearing in this guide are the property of their respective owners.

For permission requests, write to the below address:

PYP Academy Press
141 Weston Street, #155
Hartford, CT, 06141

The opinions expressed by the Author are not necessarily those held by PYP Academy Press.

Ordering Information: Quantity sales and special discounts are available on quantity purchases by corporations, associations, and others. For details, contact the author at www.marienazon.com

Edited by: Christina Consolino
Cover design by: Susan E. Wilcox
Makeup Artist/Photographer: Gordon Espinet
Typeset by: Medlar Publishing Solutions, Pvt., India

Printed in the United States of America.
ISBN: 978-1-951591-61-8 (paperback)
ISBN: 978-1-951591-62-5 (ebook)

Library of Congress Control Number: 2020925986

First edition, May 2021

The information contained within this book is strictly for informational purposes. The material may include information, products, or services by third parties. As such, the Author and publisher do not assume responsibility or liability for any third-party material or opinions. The publisher is not responsible for websites (or their content) that are not owned by the publisher. Readers are advised to do their own due diligence when it comes to making decisions.

The mission of the Publish Your Purpose Academy Press is to discover and publish authors who are striving to make a difference in the world. We give underrepresented voices power and a stage to share their stories, speak their truth, and impact their communities. Do you have a book idea you would like us to consider publishing? Please visit PublishYourPurposePress.com for more information.

PYP Academy Press
141 Weston Street, #155
Hartford, CT, 06141

Dedication

*To my mother, Lexide L. Nazon, my father,
Ouest J. Nazon, my grandmothers, Lexilia Dorval and Sylvia Nazon.
To all my Ancestors, known and unknown. I am because they were.
To my daughter, Ébun Zoule, the greatest gift of my life.*

And in loving memory of my sister friend, Amy Boyd.

Table of Contents

Foreword xii

Introduction xv

What a Woman Wants… 1

Notes 41

Acknowledgements 46

List of Co-Creators 48

Resources 49

About the Author 52

Foreword

It was in the midst of one of our life-giving Women's Belly and Womb gatherings, among nearly one hundred women dressed in shades of red who were dancing wildly with each other to the sound of the drums, that I remember finding her. She was crumpled over in grief. Kneeling before her, I looked into her eyes and asked with genuine care, "What is it? What do you need, sister?"

She cried even louder until words flew like sparks from her belly's raging inner fire. "It is not what I need!" she shouted over the rhythm. "It is what I want! Until this day I have never seen the world as I would have wanted it to be as a woman, not even a glimmer. This beauty, these colors, this wisdom, this music and dance, these children and teenagers cared for, this aliveness in all of us, this love that is palpable, these ways we are interacting together right now, and me in my body! Why did it take so long to see that this is not just a dream? This is possible. Look! It is real. This is what I want for our whole world!"

Having heard this before in my nearly four decades of empowerment work with women, this collision of reunion when a woman arrives to a place where what she wants is congruent with what she is met with and what she has longed for, I instinctually opened my arms wide. She leaned in, and I cradled her tenderly, whispering in her ear, "Welcome home, sis." She laughed, and in the next shared heartbeat, we began to dance.

This homecoming is what Dr. Marie Nazon wants for you in these pages as you may also question for yourself: What do I want? If she asked the question more specifically, such as what do you want for the world, what do you want in policies, what do you want for your family, your children, your daughter, your loved ones, the earth, what do you want to be different, what do you want as your legacy.... any number of doorways would open to layers upon layers of vision, possibility, and care where your heart, your soul, and your mind come alive. Think of us who wrote not as a monolith but as a chorus of single voices reverberating in the collective in a fraction of time. Like this round of one hundred responses, you may find yourself nodding your head, laughing, and even shocked as you think to yourself that these are really good ideas. They are pathways, revelations, fleeting thoughts, landscapes, desires, missives, musings, seeds to take on the wind, spoken simply and succinctly in a practice of raw vulnerability and honesty. This time she simply asks us to fill in spontaneously, without overthinking, what a woman wants.... (And to be fair, Marie also told us about her erotic poetry night in Harlem using this prompt and giving way to juicy thoughts as we arrived to our line that set us to wondering about our own steamy desires.)

Marie is a force, and she also happens to be one of my favorite human beings on the planet. You can hear her heart in her laughter and see it in her eyes, and when she goes belly-to-belly with you, she invites you in to meet her Ancestors as relatives by declaring: "You are my sister from another mother." Everyone who knows her will back me up that it is no exaggeration to say she is living five lives in one. She is ceaseless using every bit of her life-force in service, in caring for those she loves, for bringing visions alive, in holding hearts with care, being the priestess, teacher, wisewoman, lover, mother, friend, artist, activist, visionary... sometimes to the point of exhaustion. We all exhale when she takes a break. And still she persists. You know she will always have your belly and your back, and this comes like fierce grace wrapped in her unassuming humility. Her devotion for most of us is nearly unimaginable, and her yes often means with it, "You too."

Like a river she will pull you into the currents of her visions of what is possible. This is why you are holding answers from her wide net of sister friends spanning the globe, because when she asks us to do something, invites us to her want, there is not a one of us who would dare to say no. This makes me laugh out loud, but it is true. Who would say no to her? We trust her with our very lives. Come to think of it, if Marie wants something—and she wants it bad enough—she goes for it and makes it real, which is something we all need to think about. She might have given you not only a question to lean into but a call to live it out until it is reality, until you remember that it was always yours to begin with. And if you forget, you can look here and find yourself nodding your head and saying out loud, "Yes, please. I want what she's having."

"What is at risk for you to be the creative, alive force of love that you were born to be? What holds you back? What every day lies coerce you not to fly high, even to stay lowly in a place that betrays everything your soul is beckoning you to be? This is the moment. This is the life. This is the breath. No one can take the action you are waiting and waiting and waiting to take but you, even when others have told you "Yes you can" or "No you cannot." You decide. A thousand years from now, will anyone remember you? Perhaps not even in a hundred. So why not? Be the daring unrecorded history that mattered because you lived." **ALisa Starkweather**

Introduction

"When one woman stands, she is never alone"

–Amanda Gorman

I love women! I love men too. But my sister friends and sister circles are my medicine. They have supported me long after the guy has left, as well as in unexpected hours. My sisters are my breath, my water, the ground I walk on, and the wind beneath my wings when I need to fly. They have my belly and my back...and I have theirs. My sisters are some badass women!

For the past three decades, my physical and spiritual healing have been in communion with women circles. I am fortunate to have sister friends across the globe. Whatever place in the world I called home, I looked for, found, and created sisterhood. Long before Oprah made the term popular, my sister friends Doris, Amy, Rosita, and I co-founded a sister circle in Harlem in the early 1990s. The four of us and a few other sisters—including my blood sisters who periodically joined us—gathered monthly, providing each other with support, laughter, comfort, and healing.

My daughter grew up in circles of women, and my first sister circle helped me attract her dad. Another sister circle, the Women of Color Healing Circle, and my sisters from my Lakota sweat lodge community supported me in healing my womb to call her forth into being. As my belly grew, and as I labored and gave birth, my sisters were there. My daughter grew up surrounded by "aunties" who loved her and still do, unconditionally.

What a Woman Wants... started as a writing prompt in a creative writing class. As I filled pages and pages with *my* desires from the prompt "What a woman wants..." my curiosity about what my sisters desired increased. Inspiration struck me: reach out to my sister circles and sister friends and invite them to share a line with me using the same prompt. Some sent in one line, others two, and some lines read more like short poetry and manifestos. I relished reading all the lines that filled my inbox and was moved by the passion and vulnerability of my sisters' desires. Soon, realization overtook me: their desires matched my own, those that had not yet been verbalized. Over one hundred women, ranging in age from twenty-three to eighty-one and spanning four continents, contributed to this work. Women came from different ethnic and racial backgrounds, with varied social, economic and sexual orientation.

This project demanded to be born, and I midwifed it into being. Careful time and consideration were taken to maintain the authentic voice of each contributor. I positioned each line to flow and generated a sequence to create a melody, an aesthetic, spiritual, multidimensional experience for the reader. I had a specific vision for the cover, and thanks to the artistry of longtime friend Susan Wilcox, we made that vision come to life. The title of the book was a done deal, but I labored over the subtitle, ultimately hoping to convey the deep spiritual significance of every word in the book. The subtitle reflects the many themes that arose from the lines: sovereignty, empowerment, and erotica being most prevalent. Relationships with the self and others (including the relationship with the planet), what women want the world to look like, their roles in the world, intimate relationships, spirituality, and equity round out the rest.

I belong to sister circles of African, African American, Black Caribbean and Native American heritage, a circle of mostly Latina sisters, and circles predominantly made up of white women. For me, the joy of this project has been to finally bring my sister circles together in a literal way, reproducing my sister circles where everyone has a say, sharing their joys, struggles, and desires as a collective, modeling matriarchy where their powerful voices are not in competition for resources. My original intention was to share these desires at an open mic night, but the desires are too powerful and profound to limit them in that way. I felt an obligation to share with the world the depth and richness of women circles and desires.

Too many women have wounds that come between them, and the myth exists that we cannot all be friends. Too many women are hungry for connection. Sister circles are healing those wounds and feeding our spirits, and in that space, we call each other friends. Women have more power together than alone, and when we come together, we heal each other. This book contains that women wisdom and a vision of the world coming together.

An old gospel song was shared with me by one of my mentors as this book made her way out of the birthing canal, *This Joy* by Shirley Caesar, revitalized by the Resistance Revival Chorus – "This joy that I have, the world didn't give it to me and the world can't take it away." And it repeats itself, this strength, this peace, this love. The song spoke to my soul because it places our wants in our sovereignty. The want, whatever it is, is ours. We have grace and the power of our voice to manifest what it is we want...the world didn't give it me and the world can't take it away.

A word about the pronouns used in the book. My daughter has been my teacher in this regard, and I will admit I am still learning. I go by she/her. I chose the license to use she/her and woman throughout the book. This is not out of disrespect for those who choose other pronouns and identifiers. This book is for women who choose to call themselves a woman, whether they were born with a vagina or not. This is for anyone who espouses the Divine Feminine energy and what that means to them.

How to Use This Book

Use this book for inspiration, dreaming and taking action. Each line is from a deep place of wisdom and curiosity. You can read the book straight through, or my preference is to open the book to a random page to see who wants to speak to you. Read the top line "A woman wants..." and let your eyes rest on a line. Remember. Connect. Be inspired.

May these words move you as they have moved me.

Marie

"Well-behaved women seldom make history."

–Laurel Thatcher Ulrich

A woman wants

… to be heard and understood.

… what she wants, when she wants it, without apology or justification.

… her man to look at her like she's a plate of oxtail with extra gravy.

… to feel special and appreciated.

… to be infused with full serenity breath.

… to be alone in the bathroom for fifteen minutes without her partner, child, or pet interrupting her.

… to walk braless on the street and have it be no big thang!!!

… peace and calm in this hectic and increasingly troubled world.

… to be kissed and touched by a woman, to feel emotionally safe, sexually safe, attended to when needed à la night nurse, and lastly, family and community.

A woman wants

... to know that she is beautiful and precious without needing someone else to tell her.

... to forgive herself for self-inflicted wounds.

... to rest without worries clouding her mind.

... the remembrance of Elders gathered under the moonlight.

... love.

... to shed the layers of responsibility and dance naked in the rain under the full moon.

... a slow, sensual foot massage and to have each of her toes sucked.

... to be valued in the amount she is worth.

... an end to misogyny, patriarchy, male supremacy, and androcentrism.

... affection in long strokes.

What a woman wants is to be free from all societal restrictions, free from all insecurities she carries from girlhood, and to walk boldly and unashamedly about the earth with her titties bouncing, and her hips jiggling, and her soul singing.

A woman wants

… rest.

… honesty.

… you to know her favorite color, favorite flower, favorite song, and favorite food.

… to be her best self.

… you to love her dogs as much as you love her.

… to walk in the world, liberated and unafraid of being hassled, accosted, raped, or killed for just being her Divine self.

… a lover of her mind, protector of her soul, an admirer of her body, and someone who can appreciate her whole being.

… a man. However, that does not mean she *needs* a man.

… to live out her fantasies every day.

A woman wants

… authenticity, intentionality.

… to be waited on hand and foot.

… for the world to know there is no difference between a man and a woman.

… a firm touch.

… a balance between solitude and community.

… joy!

… a fulfilling life.

… to be touched softly, oh so softly, like a secret summer breeze that shimmers suddenly through every—yes, every—molecule of her being. An ecstatic opening. Yes! Opening!

… to BE who she truly is with no apologies.

What a woman wants is
for us to get the **preciousness of all life** on earth,
 the true gift of every heartbeat, and to tenderly and
wisely care for the children out of a deep love
 and our connection to one another
 in a sacred commitment
 to show up here fully with our courage to heal all
 of this insufferable human trauma.
Let this be a song that every soul recognizes in themselves
as we lean into the
 "Yes."

A woman wants

... to bless Our Mother Earth.

... soft kisses that become hungry, urgent kisses when the mood is right, and no one sees.

... a sharp blue spiritual flame.

... space to move, stretch and to be slow and create.

... a room of her own.

... to freely express the love she's here to gift.

... to play and shine without shame or burden from the entitled and the thirsty.

... to be loved in all her perfect imperfections.

... no debt and children who appreciate her sacrifices.

... freedom to own her own skin.

A woman wants

... tantalizing, tasty lovers.

... to be seen.

... to experience ecstasy, pleasure, and delight in her living.

... a lipstick shade that coordinates well with smashing the patriarchy.

... one more last dance with her father.

... oneness with her divinity.

... complete agency in work and in the world.

... to be in sacred space with other women.

... to be equal.

... to fill the world with her laughter, smiling widely and belly shaking.

... you to tell her no lies and say goodbye when it's over.

What a woman wants is to know her paths,

to really be able to **step into her full power**

while contributing to,

listening to, and being in concert with community.

What a woman wants is to

turn this fucked-up, upside-down world around

so that the center of our

breath (the Amazon) is not burning and plundered;

our water is clean

and abundant,

not used to flush our waste down the toilet

or cool the massive digital highway that distracts us

from what is important,

that our connection to each other, other species,

and **our Ancestors** is

strong and vibrant.

A woman wants

… a man to sit his ass down and listen.

… deep intense passion!!!

… her partner to stop putting theirself first and not get upset when she puts herself first.

… to be understood, loved unconditionally, spoiled with gifts, and accepted for all she is.

… to mess up a clean, freshly made bed.

… to be kissed passionately.

… honest and clear communication.

… to be powerful and in control, and when she handles a situation, to not be called a bitch.

… a co-conspirator, with an ease for laughing together.

A woman wants

… to feel beautiful, powerful, and wanted.

… an unlimited, unrestricted credit card with no monthly bills.

… a higher level of consciousness.

… a voice that can be heard and attended to.

… to feel overcome with safe, passionate love, engulfed in her lover's full embrace.

… to be adored.

… to be happy.

… a gentle touch from the one she loves.

… to courageously walk on the earth and feel safe.

… equal pay for equal work.

What a woman wants is **to be loved unconditionally**
And to be respected by her partner.
To experience commitment in a relationship
that manifests seamlessly!
To share a **spiritual** bond
that overrides the physical need of the flesh.

What *a woman wants is to* **not be engendered and enslaved or homogenized** *by all the archetypical shit with which society has colonized her body and mind.*

All she wants is to meet partners, friends, and family that see she is a **Divine** *Self Expression of Herself.*

A woman wants

… to be asked if she needs help.

… to feel that her lover's thirst for her is unquenchable
and to have it demonstrated to her each day.

… to be treated as God's Gift in all her confidence
and in her insecurities, in her strengths and in her weaknesses.

… orgasmic births.

… to live her life freely and unapologetically.

… her nipples sucked, like you suck on
a grape-flavored, twin popsicle.

… outrageous joy, where she is so joyous, her head hurts.

… to be worshipped.

… someone to pick her up, no questions asked,
when she breaks into a million pieces.

A woman wants

... to feel full.

... to be praised and protected.

... you to fry her some chicken and make peach cobbler from scratch.

... wild laughter that rolls out of her soul.

... to be liberated from beliefs that limit her
powerful mind, body, and spirit.

... to be worshipped and seen as the goddess she embodies.

... liberation for all people.

... a caring, sensitive companion with slow, loving hands.

... options to be serious or silly and to be respected either way.

... practical shoe compliments from other women
affirming comfort over competition.

What a woman wants is to be in **joy**

to have a world where we no longer fear the other

to feel wanted

to grow gracefully into old age

to learn to say no without feeling guilty.

What a woman wants is to know that **she matters**

that she is important to her loved ones.

that she was the best **Mom** possible

and made a positive impact on her children.

She showed them what love is and how to love;

she gave them the protection they needed and the

push and encouragement to stretch and grow and to

fly.

A woman wants

... to fall in love with her thighs.

... deep connections.

... to be held with open arms.

... those she loves to show up. To mirror her own self-worth and ability to be loved and cared for unconditionally.

... her man to clean up, be compassionate, and wash out the bathtub when finished with it.

... freedom to be all things.

... to end the patriarchal system and see the rise of the matriarchal system.

... to see and feel the glory and goodness of being a woman reflected in every aspect of her world.

... ecstatic creativity.

A woman wants

… to be accepted for everything she is and everything she is not. Only then can she step into her greatness and become the woman she is meant to be.

… solitude, a chance to collect herself.

… you to brag about her even if she is not around.

… to laugh loudly and often.

… the freedom to live life unapologetically, without fear or judgment.

… to bathe in her man's ecstasy, smearing it all over her face and breasts while licking his cream from her forearms with her tongue.

… freedom from the bonds and constraints that society has put on her and to do as she pleases without criticism or judgment.

… to spread the resources hoarded by too many to those with too little.

What a
   Woman
      Wants is
         to be seen, heard, loved

         and valued by her partner.

         Someone who will be there for her no matter what.

         A partner to live life with—to go on adventures,

         explore, create,

         and to enjoy each moment

         we have.

What a woman wants is a companion who is both a lover and friend; unconditional love, respect, and loyalty; someone to have fun with, to talk to, to share her ups and downs with

to be with someone she respects, who is her intellectual equal but that she can dance through life with

someone who inspires her and makes her life better than if she were alone; someone affectionate, not afraid of intimacy and love.

A woman wants

… someone tuned-in enough to understand what she wants before she has to ask.

… to feel confident and comfortable in her skin without validation from others.

… to release cultural indoctrination and live as her original self intended.

… the power to stop the horror inflicted by the legacy of the Trump Administration, both here and abroad.

… to receive hugs and kisses regularly.

… the support to fill up her whole space.

… her children to pick up their shit and clean up after themselves.

… freedom and support.

… to be adorned.

A woman wants

… to remember that she has the power all along.

… community composed of sisters.

… you to be fiscally responsible and pay your fair share.

… ascension.

… to be with someone who will surprise her with baseball tickets when she gets home from work.

… to have a man really *listen* to her, not just come around because he wants to sleep with her.

… you to not blink an eye when she asks for a gold bracelet.

… a kiss so passionate, she suddenly recalls her dreams from the night before.

… support, exuberance, and encouragement to explore what brings her joy and pleasure.

What a woman also wants is

a livable climate for the children's children's children

no families separated, no kids in cages

to be able to say yes more than NO NO NO

to what's going on in the world

an equitable and just transition

the meek to inherit a *living* earth (ASAP)

deep removal/healing of the psyche and culture that chooses

separation, scarcity, abuse,

domination.

What a woman wants is not to take care of her partner,
Is freedom,
Is for everyone to love her own body
Is easeful living.

A woman wants

... to realize her full potential.

... you to get down on your knees and tell her
how fucking good she looks.

... the right to walk in her spiritual sovereignty, to have the freedom
for her wings to expand as far and wide as possible.

... you not to be scared that she is a *witch*.

... you to hold her after sex.

... mutual respect.

... to be loved with all her imperfections.

... to be able to do what she wants without critique from a man.

... to be desired, caressed, and adored for her mind.

... to be treated equally.

A woman wants

… someone to hold her when she's feeling sexy
and to be at her beck and call.

… a long-lasting kiss that leads to an orgasm.

… the feathery touch of a lover's eyes witnessing her glory while
she cums multiple times, moaning a river between her thighs.

… to stand for herself as much as she stands for her children.

… Sisterhood.

… her equal.

… to fully embody her Divine soul and celebrate her luminous spirit.

… lovers who worship at the altar of her Yoni. Daily.

… you to show her off.

… harmony with nature.

What a woman wants is to be with

womyn loving womyn…

those who celebrate their own bodies as sacred

and whole no matter what.

What a woman wants is to rename herself as *Womoon* among

the wild Sistren, dancing with the power of her bloods,

the *Cauldron of Creation.*

What a woman wants is a woman who awakens

and meets her

soul embodied self,

who celebrates and is enlivened by my blossoming

as she is to hers, whose touch sends electricity
up and down my spine,

who is in for the co-creation of joy, pleasure,

earth honoring and depth-filled living.

A woman wants

… your tongue dancing inside her until she begs for more.

… stiletto and kitten heels.

… to walk as a sexually sovereign woman.

… soft light and soft voices for soft moments.

… CHOICE.

… to feel empowered and powerful and to empower others!

… to feel most special.

… to fall back into the strongest, darkest arms on Earth, into a dream world of magic and bliss, her lover catching her in his steadfast embrace.

… to have Divine Spirit and Love!

A woman wants

… her man to see wonder in her eyes, possibilities on her lips, and home in her arms.

… a partner who loves strolling with her in the park, dancing in the dark, and finding new ways to light her spark.

… to sit blissfully in nature and feel connected to Mother Earth.

… to be held and caressed until she falls asleep.

… to feel desired just as she is!

… not to be asked to smile to make someone else feel comfortable.

… to thrive, live her best life, and help everyone she loves and to leave a legacy through her work and her children.

… just *to be*—no excuses, no explanation, and no apologies. Ever!

… to have her fragrant Bat Cave to enter when she needs and/or wants it.

What a woman wants is a **seat at the table** with those

who are making decisions for her life,

her community, and the world. She wants to be where

the action is and not relegated to being in the kitchen

cooking, baking, and making babies.

She is capable of that and so much more.

A woman wants the opportunity to prove that she is more than

able to change the world and will make

no apologies for it!

What a woman wants is one man's mouth wrapped around her **clit**, another latched onto her nipple, and yet another **diving deep** into her **pussy** with his perfectly shaped, seven-and-a-half-inch, hard cock.

A woman wants

... to decide for herself what behaving is.

... to remember that Prince Charming is checking off boxes on his own to-do list.

... to experience her strength, passion, and power through the cycles of her life.

... the safety to be her authentic self.

... the desires of her heart, which may fluctuate from day to day and experience to experience and relationship to relationship.

... her partner to worship her body so intensely he can hardly believe he is worthy of such a blessing.

... to be loved just as she is, from the roots of her hair to the soles of her feet.

... peace in the world.

... to be the last thing on your mind as you close your eyes.

A woman wants

... to be licked all over—and I mean *all* over—
in the secret and not-so-secret places.

... a hot bath prepared by you on a cold night.

... sovereignty.

... to be like wild roots that twist and turn,
digging deeper and deeper.

... to listen to only one voice in her head—her own.

... for every part of her body to be cherished
and loved and respected.

... to emanate balance, peace, and wholeness.

... to be heard, not just in the sense of hearing
but to REALLY be heard.

... soft, silky butter melting on her hot skin.

What a woman wants is

the feeling of mama earth under her belly the

song of creation bubbling up in laughter

the right to love who she wants when she wants in the way she wants

so long as they want it too.

sun and wind and rain caressing her body

acknowledgment that her sensuality and passion emerge

from roots in soil, sun on body, song in heart, thick kinetic spirit

kinship between beings, most not human

to feel held in community—spirit activist diverse rich and messy complex

loving community—in real time, in the day-to-day, locally

without electronics so often mediating the connection

a worldwide turning

The sound of hummingbird wings in early morning

the peace and power of knowing she is

playing her role in transformation and healing and

what she is doing and who she is, is enough.

Knowing, with all her heart, that she is enough.
But she still want stronger shoulders.

A woman wants

… her man to say "I'm sorry" when he is wrong.

… her skin to be read like braille.

… sweet words whispered in her ears, security in his arms, equality by his side, and to create and build a legacy as partners.

… to own every room she steps into.

… a partner who is willing to stand unabashedly naked in front of her, not only in body but more importantly, in soul.

… to know the depth of her truth and share that with the world.

… one night of "freakdom," or maybe two.

… to be desired, caressed, and adored for her mind.

… forever magical moments, the kind in which fear doesn't exist.

… a man who insists on the best for her.

A woman wants

… to be held tight.

… honor and respect.

… to feel appreciated and loved for imperfections and perfections.

… power: for herSelf and for each and everyOne.

… to love deeply and be loved deeply.

… time.

… you to man-up in all things, in all situations.

… her man to hold her hand in such a way that says,
"I'm loving you and in this for the long haul."

… R-E-S-P-E-C-T.

… everything!

A woman wants

… to not be the calendar, hold all the knowledge
of other people's lives, and answer the question
"What do you think?" when it's not actually a question.

… is for women to remember we are not just living
on the earth, the earth is living through us.

… is to live knowing so we and those who come after us
can live in the TRUTH that heaven is on earth.

… sensible shoes for sexy adventures.

… to be asked what she wants.

Here is a place to write the lines that brought deep yes, hmmmm moments that made you smile, take a pause, reflect, and to write what it is you want.

Visuals are powerful tools for manifestations. Draw here what you want, your heart desires.

Acknowledgements

"It takes a village."

This gathering of women wisdom celebrates sisterhood, a sacred bond. It could not have been possible without the words and energy of my sister friends. I reached out and they responded overwhelmingly. In deep gratitude, beloveds, for saying YES to my vision. Deepest gratitude to my sister circles; the New York Sister Circle, the Women of Color Healing Circle, Roots Medicine Sisters – Priestess Path, Generation 14, and Triple Spiral Dún na Sidhe – Priestess Practicum II. Thank you to my daughter, Ébun, who is the inspiration for everything that I do. She is the manifestation of all my dreams, my walking prayer, my muse. My parents, Ouest and Lexide Nazon, my prayer warriors, now Ancestors, who taught me how to pray, encouraged me to be my best self and to "Aim High!" They continue to surround me with their love and guidance. My blood sisters who are also my best friends, Sylvia Nazon and Yanick Demund, thank you for loving me unconditionally. I am blessed to have you as my sisters *and* my friends. I adore you! Thank you to the Divine Elana Bell, in whose Sacred Expression Workshop this project was birthed. Thank you for your encouragement, loving support, and for creating a safe space for me for me to just be. And look what came out! To the brilliant Dr. Ramona Perez, who saw the beauty and possibilities of this project and midwifed me during the gestation. Her insights, expertise, and enthusiasm were significant to the development of this book. I am extremely grateful for her coaching.

I am surrounded by amazing, generous, loving people, my extended family I call my village. My village is the balm and healing of my soul and span the globe, too many to name. They are the foundation of this book. I am especially grateful for the members of my first sister circle, Doris Prester, Amy Boyd, and Rosita Timm, my village sisters, Zanetta Addams-Pilgrim, Vanessa Tricoche, Dr. Sharon McKenzie, Dr. Alice Shepard, Mary Wowk, Stephanie Kane, Susan Wilcox, my brothers from another mother, Raymond Rodriguez, Jonathon Moon, Gordon Espinet, and Jonathan Ledoux. Katrina Jeffries for her helpful insights on the layout and for reminding me of my greatness. My Momentum family, LT177 and Advance, who held me accountable to complete this project.

Thank you Publish Your Purpose Press, especially the founder and CEO Jenn Grace for her generosity and for being my cheerleader during the last stages of the process. Thank you to Bailly and my fellow writers at the Academy for your generous feedback. Publish Your Purpose Academy helped me bring my vision to fruition.

Finally, special thank you to my spiritual teachers and mentors for sharing their wisdom and showing me a way of being that serves my highest self. I have learned so much from them, and they continue to nourish my spirit: Esperanza Martell, founder of the Women of Color Healing Circle. It all started with you! ALisa Starkweather, Makhosi Gogo Ateyo Nkanyezi, thank you for pushing me for my highest good even when it is so uncomfortable for me, Gina Martin, Babalawo Ifagbemi Musafa, Kumu Leihulu Iwi'ula, Mambo Jocelyne Dorestan, Ann Benedetto, Beverly Little Thunder, Hilda Marie, Rev. Julie MacDonald, Norma Margot, Alicia Holmes, and my brother Yves F. Nazon (Baba Ifasegun).

In deep gratitude.

Àṣẹ!

List of Co-Creators

Sherley Accime / Zanetta Addams-Pilgrim / Lise Afoy / Adeyinka M. Akinsulure-Smith, PhD / Grace Aldrich / Jennifer Atlee / Myriam Augustin / Aviva B. / Amy Bauman / Elana Bell / Pascale Bernard / Stephanie Berry / Teagan Blackburn / Emily Blefeld / Amy Boyd / Celia Bracy / Ginny Brooke / Victoria Brosnan / Kisha T. Bundrige / Robin G. Burdulis / Laura C / Annie Chang / Joan Checca / Katie Maguire Chiaravolloti / Colleen Gorman / Kate C. / Kerry Colville / Laura Lula Delano / Malinda DeMercurio / Julissa Dilone / Olivia Drouhaut / Shénae Dure / Netlyn Bernard / AF / Rhea Faniel / Alexandra Gialaboukis / Kat Gibson / Marsha Gildin / Leandra J / Asia Jean / Jill A / Gena Jefferson / Katrina Jeffries / Margaret Harris / Heartsmind / Tracey Hebert-Seck / Tracy Hobson / Alicia Holmes / Queen Italina / Zenzele Isoke / ILOV GRATE / Stephanie Kane / Lisa Kirsch / Anna Kramer / Carolina Kroon / Melanie L. / Monique Lang / Jodi Lasseter / Connie Leeper / Lyris / Beverly Little Thunder / Iris Lopez / Magdalena Lopez / Tracy Louis / Kara Lynch / Julie MacDonald / Elena Mansour / Hilda Marie / Gina Martin / Esperanza Martell / Dr. McKenzie / Bailey Carter Moulse / Brinda Nazon / Deborah Nazon / Sylvia Nazon / Ébun Nazon-Power / Cosette Nazon-Wilburn / Taylor Nazon / Yanick Nazon / Tiffany Nelson / Makhosi Gogo Ateyo Nkanyezi / Shawnteeha Patterson / Dr. R.L. Perez / Marcela Petric / Doris Prester / Merelis Catalina Ortiz / Kim Roberts / Flash Rosenberg / Kyesha Ruffin / Katie S. / Irijah Stennett / Akasha S. / Nonty Sabic / Carol Smith / Lynette Smith / Tej Rae / ALisa Starkweather / Stacey Toro / Mother Turtle / Lanita Summerlin / Dyan Summers / Rosita Timm / Catrina Toole / Vanessa Tricoche / Maelinda Turner / Donna Wilding / Karen Wadsworth / Susan E. Wilcox / Zoe Williams / Dina Wolleben / Nariya Worrell / Lona Jack-Vilmar / Marian Zeitlin

Resources

Your Voice is Our Gift: Women and Girls

Ashe Birthing Services: https://www.ashebirthingservices.com
Bitcoin Bombshell: https://www.bitcombomshell.com
Black and Pink Pen Pals: https://blackandpinkpenpals.org
Black Feminist Futures: https://www.blackfeministfuture.org/our-vision
Black Women Blue Print: https://www.blackwomensblueprint.org
Black Girls Code: https://www.blackgirlscode.org
Brujas of Brooklyn: https://www.brujasofbrooklyn.com
Center for Anti-Violence Education: https://www.caeny.org
Center for Reproductive Rights: https://www.reproductiverights.org
Dear Grown Ass Women: https://www.deargrownasswomen.com
FIERCE: https://www.fiercenyc.org
Fistula Foundation: https://www.fistulafoundation.org
Girl Trek: https://girltrek.org
Girls Auto Clinic: https://girlsautoclinic.com
Girls for Gender Equity: https://www.ggenyc.org
Global Sisterhood: https://www.globalsisterhood.org
Hire My Mom: https://www.hiremymom.com
Hour Children: https://www.hourchildren.org
JAIA Youth Empowerment: https://jaiayouth.org

Journey to Wealth: Instagram @wealthywomanmagic

Latinas and Lideres: Latinaslideres.com; Instagram: @LatinasLideres

Love My Womb Academy: https://lovemywombacademyonline.com

Malala Fund: https://Malala.org

Mothers On The Move: https://mothersonthemove.org

Movement Generation: https//www.movementgeneration.org

Planned Parenthood: https//www.plannedparenthood.orf

Princess Chambers, Inc: https://princesschambersinc.org

Rape, Abuse, and Incest National Network: https//www.rainn.org

Sister Love: https://www.sisterlove.org

Sister Sol: https://brotherhood-sistersol.org

Strengthen Our Sisters: https://www.strengthenoursisters.org

The Loveland Foundation: https://thelovelandfoundation.org

Mother Artist Salon: https://www.elanabell.com/mother-artist

The Mom Project: https://themomproject.com

Ultra Violet: https//www.weareultraviolet.org

UPROSE: https://www.uprose.org

We All Grow Latina: https://amigas.weallgrowlatina.com/feed

Willie Mae Rock Camp: https://www.williemaerockcamp.org

WomenArts: https//www.womenarts

Women's Environment & Development Organization: https://www.wedo.org

The Earth is Our Mother: Enviromental

Another Gulf is Possible: https://anothergulf.com

Earth Rights Institute: https://www.earthrightsinstitute.org

Earthseed Collective: https://www.earthseedlandcoop.org

Environmental Defense Fund: https://www.edf.org

Gaia Education: https://www.gaiaeducation.org

Greenpeace: https://www.Greenpeace.org

Kunsikeya Tamakoce: https://kunsikeya.org

Native Movement: https://nativemovement.org

Natural Resources Defense Council: https://act.nrdc.org

NC Climate Justice Collective: https//www.ncclimatejustice.info

Climate Justice Alliance: https://climatejusticealliance.org

Rally for Rivers: https://isha.sadhguru.org/rally-for-rivers

REDES – Network for Ecovillage Emergence and Development in the Sahel, Senegal: http://redes-ecovillages.org/eng

Riverkeeper: https://riverkeeper.org

Sierra Club: https://sierraclub.org/environmental-justice

Soul Fire Farm: https://www.soulfirefarm.org

Tree Sisters: https://treesisters.org

Triple Spiral Dún na Sidhe: https://www.triplespiralofdunnasidhe.net

Union of Concerned Scientists: https://www.ucsusa.org

WE ACT for Environmental Justice: https//www.weact.org

Women's Earth Alliance: https://www.womensearthalliance.org

About the Author

Marie C. Nazon, PhD, LMSW, is a social worker with over twenty-five years of clinical experience in mental health. She is a member of the counseling faculty at the City College of New York SEEK program and a practicing psychotherapist. A *Returned Peace Corps Volunteer* and former *Fulbright Scholar* in Senegal, Dr. Nazon is passionate about women's empowerment and has co-founded and led women's support circles in Africa and in New York. Grounded in indigenous spiritual wisdom, she is a *Mambo*, an initiated priestess in Haitian Vodou, and an *Iyanifa*, an initiated priestess in the Yoruba spiritual tradition of Ifa. She is also a graduate of ALisa Starkweather's Priestess Path Apprenticeship, *Generation 14*, and *Priestess Practicum* of Triple Spiral Dún na Sidhe, a pagan spiritual community. She is a member of the *Kunsi Keya Tamacoke's* Lakota Sweat Lodge, Women's Sundance community for over 25 years and a student of *O Kalama Ho'omana* Hawaiian spirituality. As a clinician/healer and *Reiki Master*, she believes in the magnificent capability of the human body and mind to heal itself. Marie lives in the village of Harlem, New York with her family and four leggeds, Jazz the cat and dog, Rumi.

www.ingramcontent.com/pod-product-compliance
Lightning Source LLC
Chambersburg PA
CBHW050751110526
44592CB00002B/27